SPACE
■S
空
間

D1486440

Shop

PACE
www.beisistudio.com

cover photo: ©Edmund Sumner

© 2008 by pace publishing limited
issn: 1022-5609-71
isbn: 978-962-7723-99-8

pace publishing limited
17/f., north point asia-pac commercial centre,
10 north point road, north point,
hong kong
t: +852 28971688
f: +852 28972888
www.beisistudio.com
pace@pacebase.com

publisher: george lam / george.lam@beisistudio.com
editorial: diane tsang / diane_tsang@pacebase.com
proofreader: maisy chan
design / layout: diane

Preface

by Agnes Lung

About Agnes Lung

Agnes Lung is a veteran marketing and brand management professional with over 12 years of solid working experience in the retail industry. She has worked for many world-renowned retail companies such as LVMH Group, Shiseido DCH Co. Ltd., L'Oreal HK Co. Ltd., and Duty Free Shoppers. She was the Chief Communications Controller for MaBelle Diamond Group and was in charge of all marketing, branding and communications strategies including shop image and design, as well as undergoing the brand revamp campaign for the brands in the company group. She has recently joined Sa Sa International Holdings Company Limited as Vice President, Marketing.

SHOP DESIGN

Over the past decade, shop retail design has become more and more predominant in many retailing businesses. Owners have come to realize the utmost importance of having professionals in shop design not only to exhibit the overall brand image of a shop in attracting customer traffic, or focusing on the practicality or functionality, but most important of all, to communicate these values in the perspective of their potential customers, i.e. what their shops stand for and how do these shops fit with the customers' personality, value, and buying behaviour.

Branding is a holistic approach in building a brand's identity, benefits and how it relates and associates to the customers' wants, and having these messages communicated effectively and consistently to our customers. Shop retail design is one of the few very key tools in conveying these messages. Instead of how an owner wants to build up an image he or she desires, today the approach is more interactive, with owners willing to outsource professional retail designers to help materialize these wishes. This trend allows brand owners to have third party expertise rather than judging the wants and needs of a customer from their own angle.

Retailing business is all about 'understanding our customers' and not 'how we think the customers are.' It is crucial to have the mindset of learning the customers' wants, how the companies/brands can fill these gaps and win loyalty from the customers. Having a third party and professional retail shop designer enable owners to achieve:

1) A shop image which demonstrates the brand identity and differentiate it from the competition,

2) Functional usage and need according to the business nature such as numbers of display area, inventory storage and so forth,

3) A shopping environment, which contributes to the 'Total Shopping Experience.'

Today, we are talking about 'Consumer Experience Management', and how can it be done without a thorough thinking on shop design here? We can easily see that major retailers understand how crucial it is to provide a pleasant shopping experience to our consumers and we have to compromise the space of having more merchandise with better ambience as well as a more interesting shopping experience, such as special waiting areas with cosy, and attention-to-detail in furniture and world class décor. The 'less is more' concept has set in even in many long established local retailers and the cooperation between a shop owner and interior designer is not only a business transaction but seeing each other as 'strategic partners' is now the emerging trend. Designers are now even more aggressive in voicing their opinions on how a brand should communicate their brand equity to consumers and very often they are also the ones who spot the future trends of these consumers and recommend the owners to further innovate as pioneers in the industries, they are able to do so since they can be more easily see things in consumers' perspective, and therefore interior designers for retail shops play an vital role in balancing the subjectivity and to provide more interactive inputs to retail owners. All retailers should work hand in hand with interior designers who share the same values in achieving the optimal business result.

Agnes Lung, 2007

Contents

104

144

8

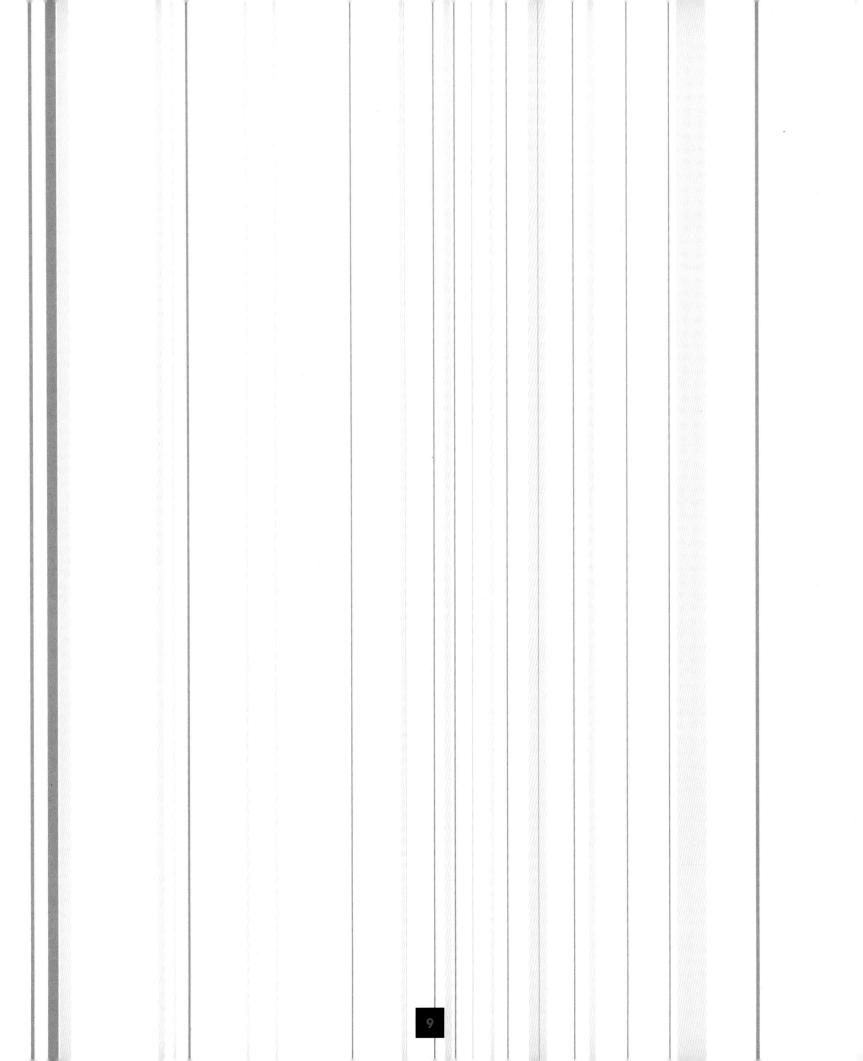

Hyundai Brandshop/Finance shop, Seoul

Concrete Architectural Associates

■ Seoul, Korea
■ Brandshop, 148 sq.m.
■ Finance Shop Seogho, 70 sq.m.
■ Finance Shop Yangjae, 65 sq.m.

The corporate identity is based on the rounded rectangle of the credit card. By extruding this rectangle and subtracting it from the given spaces, the store identity emerges.

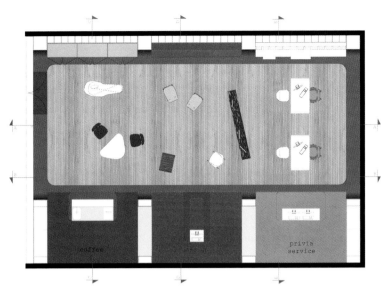

Hyundai Brandshop Floor Plan

Section A-A

Section B-B

We developed a master plan for the stores of HyundaiCard and Hyundai Capital located throughout Seoul and South Korea. These stores which offer faceted financial services are intended to tap into the highly competitive South Korean market.

On top of regular financial services, they want to add a special flavour to the store. The lounge, emerged as a private club, is exclusively created for card members and Capital customers.

We translated their existing 2D identity created by the graphic agency, Total Identity, into a 3rd dimension. The corporate identity is based on the credit card: the rounded rectangle. By extruding the rounded rectangle and subtracting it from the given spaces, the store identity emerges. We performed this on different scales, so every form within the store is consistent with the rounded rectangle, which creates a

prevailing identity. We transferred this identity onto the floor, wall, ceiling, furniture, and details.

The financial shop, which needs to be extremely customer friendly, is completely white. It has a light bamboo floor supporting the corporate coloured blue back wall. A glass wall with the sandblasted script of 'finance' divides the store into the pantry and meeting room.

One of the walls in the store contains a 3 dimensional information niche. This 3D wall is equipped with flat screens, tables and A4 format folders.

The other wall in the store carries an image of a city skyline, which represents the young, urban and professional characters of HyundaiCard and Hyundai Capital. There are three help desks

The flagship store is divided into three different sections: the coffee bar (brown), the design shop (red), and the 'privia' service (orange). At the back is a small finance shop separated by the tree trunk bench by Jurgen Bey.

furnished with white plastic Eames chairs and a white leather waiting couch.

The flagship store, which should have a more exclusive appearance, is completely black with a caramel bamboo floor. It is divided into three different sections: the coffee bar (brown), the design shop (red) and the 'privia' service (orange). We placed different classical design chairs and tables on the bamboo floor. At the back, there is a small finance shop, which is separated from the rest through the tree-trunk-bench by Jurgen Bey.

The back wall of the flagship store contains an image of a beech forest. This gives a peaceful tranquillity in contrast with the city. The back walls of the sectional spaces are graphically filled by Total Identity.

The furniture in the sections are again extruded rounded rectangles with a stainless steel inlay adjusted to the functions of the section. The ceilings in the finance shop and flagship store are made of white stretch ceilings, backlit by tube lights as general illumination. All around the ceiling surfaces, spots are placed to supply theatrical lighting.

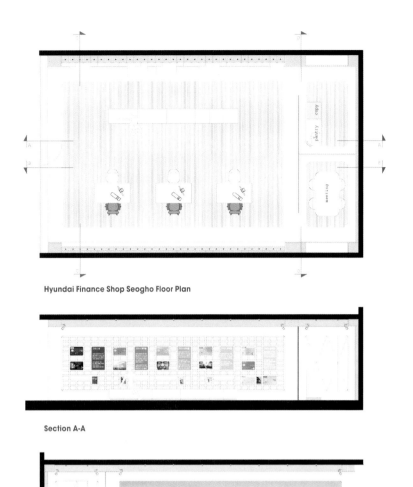

Hyundai Finance Shop Seogho Floor Plan

Finance Shop Seogho: One wall of the store contains a 3 dimensional information niche equipped with flat screens, tables and A4 format folders.

Section A-A

Section C-C

Section B-B

Section D-D

Finance Shop Yangjae: The same concept is carried into the Yanjae store, with identical furniture and similar information wall.

HyundaiCard **Hyundai Capital** **GE Partner** **Finance Shop**

Client
Hyundaicard / Hyundai Capital

Design Team
Rob Wagemans, Janpaul Scholtmeijer, Erik van Dillen, Charlotte van Mill

Consultants
Total Identity, Amsterdam
Spackman Associates, Seoul

Furniture
Eames, Prouve, Miller, Tree-trunk-bench by Jurgen Bey

Wall Covering
Steel, Glass

Ceiling
Steel

AV System
Stereo Music System and i-Pod Sound System by BOSE

Photography
Hyundaicard / Hyundai Capital

Aesop Eslite, Taipei
CJ Studio

- **Taipei, Taiwan**
- **53 sq.m.**

The design concept is "bookstore/library", and black elements from the Eslite Bookstore interior are adopted by using black iron bookshelves to display beauty products.

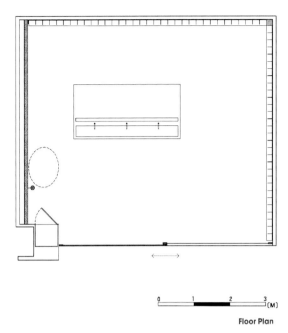

Floor Plan

Distinct from the ordinary market operation, Australian beauty brand Aesop has entered the Eslite Bookstore in the Shin-Yi district. Situated on the 2nd floor of the best-seller area, Aesop breaks the rules of cosmetic retail space planning, and boldly places the shop inside the bookstore. Customers can now purchase the beauty products while reading and selecting books.

This innovative retail positioning derives from the unique target group of Aesop. The person who comes to Eslite Bookstore loves books and art, which matches Aesop's customer base. Putting Aesop in Eslite can broaden the reading scope of the consumers, and at the same time strengthen the aesthetics in life.

The interior space is designed by Shichieh Lu, the award-winning architect who currently works with Aesop. Lu takes "bookstore/library"

as the design concept and adopts the black element from Eslite interior design by using the black iron bookshelves to display beauty products. Numerous products are lined on the shelf to create a minimalist atmosphere. Lu also uses black oak and palm tree fibre carpet to forge a calm and natural environment, which strengthens Aesop as a brand with humanitarian concerns.

Numerous products line the shelf to create a minimalist atmosphere.

Lu also uses black oak and palm tree fibre carpet to forge a calm and natural environment, which strengthens Aesop as a brand with humanitarian concerns.

Client
Dennis and Clement

Design Team
Schichieh Lu

Photography
Marc Gerritsen

Mendo, Amsterdam
Concrete Architectural Associates

■ Amsterdam, The Netherlands
■ 100 sq.m.

As bricks are the basis of a masonry house, our design is based on a plain, black, custom-designed MENDO-Book.

Mendo is all about creative books. This is why books have been the starting point of our design. The result is a bookshop built by books. As bricks are the basis of a masonry house, our design is based on a plain, black MENDO-Book we designed.

Upon entry into the shop, clients are surrounded by filigree bookshelves made of steel filled up with the black MENDO-Books. In some spots, the MENDO-Books are replaced by books sold in the shop. These display spaces create colourful gaps within the black MENDO-Book walls. This effect, and the use of adjustable spot lights draw special attention to the books on sale. The position and number of gaps are flexible and therefore can be changed to meet various promotions and activities.

Modern art, which is also sold at Mendo, is hung on the upper edge of the bookshelves using the black MENDO-Books as its background.

At the end of the bookshelves running along the whole length of the shop, a mirror wall is installed which visually doubles the length of the shelves and the entire shop.

At the centre of the shop, we placed smaller bookshelves which are "fallen over". As their vertical counterparts, they are used as a displaying background for the books. Besides, they form little islands in the shop where clients are invited to sit down, have a closer look at the books, listen to music or just relax. The chrome Bolster lamps which hang above each island create extra intimacy.

Smaller bookshelves which are "fallen over" are used as a displaying background for the books. Chrome Bolster lamps which hang above each "fallen bookshelf" create extra intimacy.

Client
Mendo

Design Team
Rob Wagemans, Lisa Hassanzadeh, Erik van Dillen

Lighting Fixtures & Fittings
Modular Lighting

Interior Carpentry
Roord binnenbouw

Furniture
Steelwork by Smederij van Rijn,

Wall Covering
Metal stud walls by Heemskerk Bouwspecialiteiten, leather tiles, colour dune, Blackstone, black painted plaster work

Flooring
Black mat resin floor by Vermeulen Kunststofvloeren

Ceiling
Black painted plaster work

Artwork
Mendo books by Drukkerij over de Linden posthuma bv

Photography
www.ewout.tv

DAVIDS Footwear Boutique, Toronto
burdifilek

■ Toronto, Canada
■ 285 sq.m.

The final interior design language is a composition of sleek architectural forms, refined volumes and spaces articulated in beautiful materials.

The 2007 spring season brought the unveiling of the new DAVIDS footwear flagship on Bloor Street in Toronto. The award winning interior design firm burdifilek reinvented the landmark retailer's environment in the same location where the DAVIDS brand has built its reputation for decades.

Behind the revitalized new ebony façade, floor to ceiling windows expose the stunning new volume of space that glows like a pristine adornment on the Bloor street landscape. burdifilek created an architectural language for DAVIDS that embraces rich tones, elaborate textures and noble form to create a refined backdrop that elevates the iconic boutique and retail experience.

The open-concept two-story space has women's footwear on the main floor and men's on the mezzanine level. The entrance to the store is announced with a monumental glass staircase gracefully articulating its way between the two floors. A matte charcoal coloured wall sculpture in a subtle corrugated texture creates a visual movement and is complemented by the smoky patina of a wood veneer that is the backdrop within the space.

The overall palette is rich in tone and texture and there is a wealth of space to let the product take centre stage. Custom seating, beautifully crafted furniture and exotic materials like Makassar wood, honed limestone and Starfire glass all play out within the space. Matte surfaces like sandblasted Lucite and suede deeply contrast shiny and reflective materials like polished steel and planes of seamless mirror.

The overall concept alludes to aristocratic, but remains absolutely progressive and modern. The final interior design language is a composition of sleek architectural forms, refined volumes and spaces articulated in beautiful materials. burdifilek's creative concept embodies the history of the half-century old brand and creates a new international aesthetic in Toronto's most exclusive shopping district.

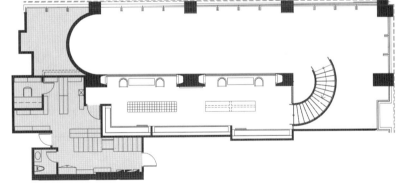

Mezzanine level floor plan

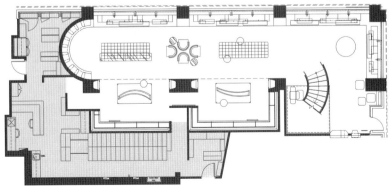

Main level floor plan

Lightbright

Mechanical/Electrical
MCW Consultants

Structural
Blackwell Bowick

Lighting Fixtures & Fittings
Litemore

Furniture
Kai Leather, Unique Store Fixtures

Wallcovering
Crown Wallpaper

Flooring
Sullivan Source

Upholstery
Fabrics by Primavera, Custom upholstery
by Creative Custom

A/V System
Bay Bloor Radio

Photography
Ben Rahn of A Frame Studio

Wai Yuen Tong, Hong Kong
Another

■ Hong Kong, China
■ 120 sq.m.

The design keeps a well-planned layout and
retains key elements of the Chinese herbal shop
such as the 'hundred herbal drawers'.

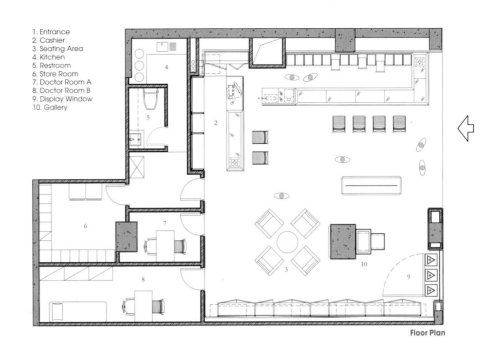

1. Entrance
2. Cashier
3. Seating Area
4. Kitchen
5. Restroom
6. Store Room
7. Doctor Room A
8. Doctor Room B
9. Display Window
10. Gallery

Floor Plan

The direction of the design was to revamp the popular Chinese herbal and medicine shop - "Wai Yuen Tong" into a fresh and contemporary store while at the same time retaining the traditional values of its unique brand identity.

To create a modern luxury store, the corporate colour of orange is applied alongside the golden stainless steel and dark timber finishes. The design keeps a well-planned layout and retains key elements of the Chinese herbal shop such as the 'hundred herbal drawers'.

The design is intended to appeal to the young generation to try out Chinese herbal remedies and to balance off the old brand name with a contemporary modern identity.

41

Client
Wai Yuen Tong

Design Team
Pal Pang

Main Contractor
C & T Contracting Ltd.

Lighting Consultant
Pal Pang

Art Consultant
Pal Pang

Photography
Another

RW & Co., Barrie
II BY IV Design Associates Inc.

■ Barrie, Canada
■ 340 sq.m.

Dramatic, dark framing is part of the new, more
modern, 'grown-up' materials and finishes.

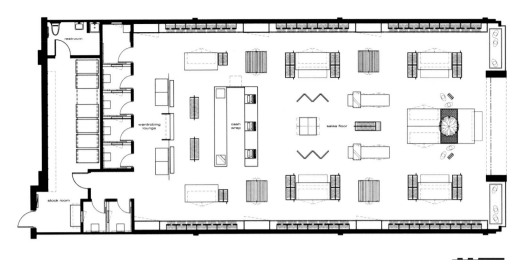

Floor Plan

This growing retail brand for men and women is a division of Reitmans (Canada) Ltd., the 80+ year-old, 1,000-store, retail leader. Launched with a series of high school and college promotions, the brand's original focus was on youthful buyers and their parents. Seven years later, management determined that there was a greater long-term profit potential in a slightly older market. The change in target market from teens to 18-30 year old career starters called for a corresponding product change, from casual club and school wear to moderately priced urban chic clothing and accessories, promoted as 'uniquely yours to fit your lifestyle'. In turn, the company called on II BY IV to create a new store design to reflect these changes and to provide a contemporary look grounded in functionality and marketing support.

The dramatically different storefront clearly announces the change in focus. The edgy angled canvas canopies and I-beam-pierced façade are gone. Instead, a strongly branded, highly visible portal offers an open and welcoming view of the store interior, framed by a dramatic dark lacquer panel in a fine-lined custom texture. The panels are repeated as graphic headers inside and the lines are referenced in the stone flooring striations as well as in a network pattern constructed in metal, inscribed on wood and sandblasted on glass in various fixtures.

Just inside the huge portal, the designers created a striking entrance feature by introducing an elegant planter and a graceful tree as part of the extensive bank of presentation tables that is so important to the chain's merchandising program.

Just inside the entry area, the designers created a striking entrance feature by introducing an elegant planter and graceful tree as part of the extensive bank of presentation tables.

Although the merchandise split is skewed to women's clothing, the designers ensured that the side wall merchandising was balanced equally between the sexes, to create a welcoming environment for male shoppers. The new design backlights graphics of attractive male and female faces, raises them for greater visibility and fronts them with presentation tables to create a powerful selling unit. For a compelling presentation of the three key groupings of perimeter merchandisers, the designers used an unusual slatted wood framing that highlights the product and graphic panels and provides a strong, gender-neutral character.

The dramatic, dark framing is part of the new, more modern, 'grown-up' materials and finishes. The layout and fixturing make the stores highly functional and easy to manage, lowering costs as well as updating the image. Bringing as much storage onto the selling floor as possible, concealed below presentation tables and behind graphic panels, reduced the back of house square footage to a minimum. In another space-stretching tactic, movable, chrome-framed divider screens, mirrored on one side and merchandised on the other, house many kinds of accessories while visually expanding and adding a lively sparkle to the central shopping area.

More sparkle results from the custom, icicle-like ceiling fixtures in sandblasted glass that enliven the cash desk and change room areas and attract customers deeper into the store. The cash desk itself is a long sleek unit with a hot-rolled steel top floating above a bright chrome reveal. The desk incorporates a brightly glowing, glass-door, self-serve, refrigerator stocked with RW-branded bottled water.

Contrasting sharply with the huge backlit posters that backdrop the cash desk, and separating it from the change area, a black ball chain screen balances privacy and transparency. Sandblasted with a huge store logo, mirrorfronted fitting rooms made the generous change area seem even larger.

Easily scaleable, the new design has been translated for big box sites with additional fixturing and the addition of a small music listening guest lounge. Brighter, more sophisticated and more open, it has proven to be a success with the target customers and landlords alike.

A strongly branded, highly visible portal offers an open and welcoming view of the store interior, framed by a dramatic dark lacquer panel in a fine-lined custom texture.

Client
Reitmans (Canada) Ltd.

Main Contractor
Belle Construction

Fixtures
Metalwork by Roy Meals
Millwork by GD Pro

Wallcovering
Metrowallcovering

Flooring
Stone Tile

Fabric
Maharam

Artwork
Tree feature by Gian Rocco

Photography
David Whittaker

STEPHANE DOUCHANGLEE YUGIN

Stephane Dou Changlee Yugin Sogo, Taipei

CJ Studio

■ Tapei, Taiwan
■ 50 sq.m.

In this store the bent, glossy stainless steel design is not only a fashion hanger but also a structural support.

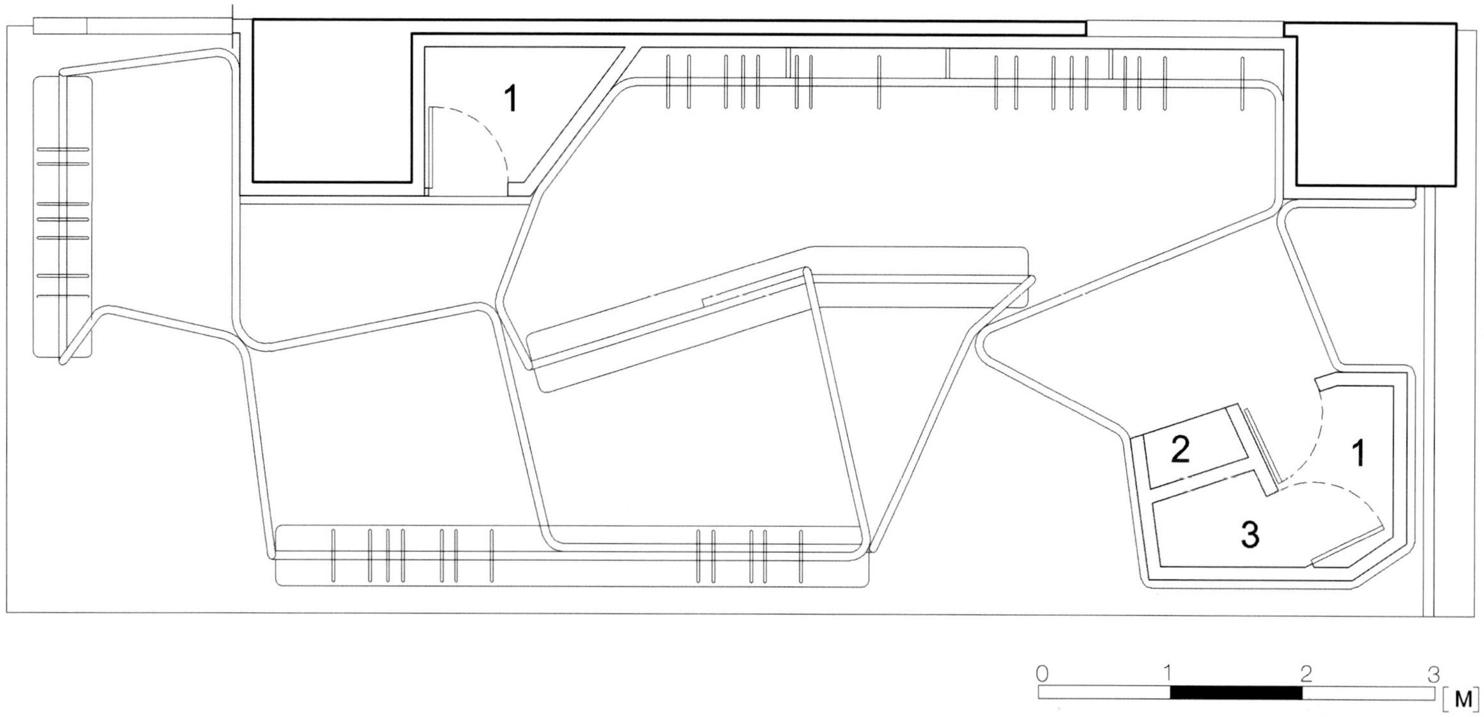

Floor Plan - 1. Change Room; 2. Counter; 3. Storage

This boutique is located at BR4 of the SOGO department store extending the same fashionable sophistication and futuristic sensation of the previous STEPHANE DOU - CHANGLEE YUGIN stores. On the other hand, it has created a unique personality in the environment. The designer used a lot of glossy stainless steel bent at specific angles, like hexagons, to create a smooth visual movement. At the same time, the white terrazzo walls that extend from the ground and hold the floating form make a perfect balance in the entire design.

It appears as a simple line throughout the whole space. In fact, the designer has to calculate every angle and its tension precisely. The bending stainless steel design is not only a fashion hanger but also a structural support. It is a display of complicated technical mastery where nails nor screws can hardly be found on the surface of the metal. With few decorations and no miscellaneous objects, it represents the pithy concept of STEPHANE DOU and CHANGLEE YUGIN brand.

Client
Stephane Dou Changlee Yugin

Design Team
Shichieh Lu, Giono Chung, Cindy Lin

Main Contractor
Zhishen International Co., Ltd.

Photography
Marc Gerritsen

apart by lowrys, Tokyo
Ichiro Nishiwaki Design Office Inc.

■ Tokyo, Japan
■ 230 sq.m.

Furniture, like sofa, desks, and shelves are all antique furniture imported from Europe which create a warm atmosphere.

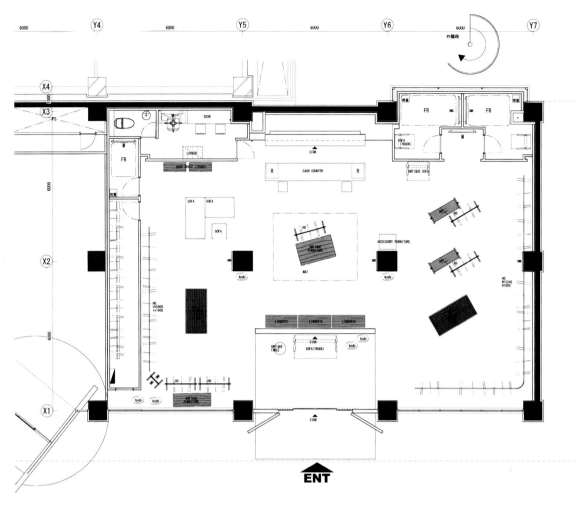

Floor Plan

"apart by lowrys" is a fashion brand targeting women in their late twenties and thirties. It offers casual but trendy fashion at a reasonable price. Established in 2006, the name was derived from "LOWRYS FARM" (a popular fashion brand targeting teenagers) and already has 12 shops in Japan. This is a flagship store located in Daikanyama, one of the hotspots for fashion, avant-garde architecture, and café culture.

As its brand name suggests, the concept of this store is "an apartment in Paris". Like an apartment house located at an alley, residents renovate rooms, floor, and walls over and over again with their personal tastes and preferences ... that is the image of "apart by lowrys".

The client, POINT INC, wanted this store to be a hand-made-style original store. So the designer selected a special painting method to express an "aging" appeal with an antique map of Paris accentuating

the wall. The entrance wall and blue signboard at the back of the counter are also painted in aging expression. At the entrance, the large antique doors are painted in rusty finish. It has a strong presence and draws people into the store. The furniture like sofas, desks, and shelves are all antique furniture imported from Europe which create a warm atmosphere.

The floor is painted white and is an original finish of this store (other stores do not have the white flooring). Nishiwaki's aim was that the white flooring will soon be worn out with customer's footprints and the store will be nearing a dated outlet with a long history.

The aim of the white floor is to be worn out with customer's footprints so the store will be nearing a dated outlet with a history.

Client
POINT INC.

Design Team
Ichiro Nishiwaki, Yoshimichi Watanabe,
Eri Yamaguchi

Main Contractor
Space

Lighting Consultant
On & Off

Lighting Fixtures & Fittings
Daiko

Furniture
Shelf and Sofa from Lloyd's Antiques

Wall Covering
Aizu

Artwork
Sculptures and mobiles by Hirotoshi
Sawada and Dennis Lin

Flooring
Gallup

Photography
Kozo Takayama

HEDDIE LOVU, Tokyo
GLAMOROUS co., ltd.

■ Tokyo, Japan
■ 78 sq.m.

Two large columns become the focal point
when they are transformed into merry-go-rounds
showcasing the products.

In line with the name "HEDDIE LOVU" which comes from Musee du Louvre, the design concept of the store is "Museum". Refining the selection as a specialized store selling top quality jeans and displaying them like museum art, customers enjoy shopping with descriptions of staff selections and trial fitting.

Inside, there is an issue with the original structure – 2 large columns visible from the outside which hinder visibility of the shop display.

The solution is to put a "spin" on the issue and create a visual point by making a merry-go-round to wrap around each column. On the merry-go-rounds, there are mannequins outfitted in jeans astride hobby horses embedded with over 30,000 pieces of crystals. The idea was to make the jeans attractive and the silhouette including

hip-lines understandable by showcasing the bodyline of products as the merry-go-round move.

The idea behind the embedded crystals is that they sparkle with elegance, and are gorgeous and bright like no other material. The brightness also illuminates the shiny black frames on the wall creating a double effect of the shop's glamour.

The essence of all design materials is to process and install them to bring out the whole design in its entirety. By doing so, the space would be functional and attractive, accentuated with its unique characters.

"When I am working on a design, I always have the space in my mind and walk around the 'mind map' as if I were the customer

or staff of the shop. I have never designed a shop for 'cool' or 'trendy' sensations. But I believe a space in which everyone feels 'comfortable' and 'friendly' will be a preferred space regardless of time. It is not a 'trendy store', but a 'thriving shop'," – Yasumichi Morita.

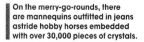

On the merry-go-rounds, there
are mannequins outfitted in jeans
astride hobby horses embedded
with over 30,000 pieces of crystals.

Client
Restir. Inc.

Design Team
Mr. Yasumichi Morita, Mr. Daisuke
Watanabe

Main Contractor
Tanseisya Co., Ltd.

Lighting Consultant
Mr. Kenji Ito of Maxray Inc.

Lighting Fixtures & Fittings
Ceiling-Down light by Maxray Inc.
Fitting room-Pendant fixture by
watts(Olbia 7001p)

Furniture
Display table – custom made (Wood
painted in black)

Wall Covering
Clear mirror, Fixed flames (non-flammable
moulding material painted in black + clear
mirror with smoked sheet + sheet of iron
with black suede panel)

Ceiling
Acrylic emulsion paint

Flooring
Mortor + stone

Merry-go round
Base-Stainless steel(black baking paint)
Column- Stainless steel(black baking
paint) with 100,000 black and hematite
crystal glass chips.

Hobby Horse
Shiny ziehl black burning + crystal, FRP
shinyblack urethane coating. Crystal
is swarovski component flatback
/No.2028/4.6/JET, hematite

Photography
Nacasa & Partners Inc.

La Cité Shopping Mall, Liaoning
JBM Design

■ Liaoning, China
■ 5,000 sq.m.

The double height ceiling with custom designed pendant lights at the entrance bring elegance and sophistication to the space.

La Cité department store is located at Dandong City of Liaoning, which is in the north east of China. The client approached the designer and stated that they wanted to create a store that makes customers feel like they were in the Champs Elysées.

This is a challenging project. The designer has to introduce and implement the most contemporary international shopping standards and environment to consumers who live in this city and nearby North Korea.

The difficulty was the implementation of our design in this city, the required workmanship, and quality material sourcing, etc. The designer also took into consideration its geographical location and relative climatic factors.

The premise is a very old 2-storey building. The designer reconstructed the front façade into a completely transparent shop front, bringing a fresh and dynamic outlook to the city yet at the same time maintaining the original building structure. The focal point is the double height ceiling with custom designed pendant lights at the entrance which brings elegance and sophistication to the space.

The designer's basic idea was the total quality, elegance, exaltation, and physiological reference to marks and materials. The designer intended to make this bulky place harmonious and able to stimulate visual and sensorial perception.

Client
La Cité

Design Team
Michael Chan

Photography
JBM Design

MISCH MASCH, Osaka
Ichiro Nishiwaki Design Office Inc.

- Osaka, Japan
- 185 sq.m.

The heart-shaped chandelier consists of limestones and Swarovski crystals with CDM light sources creating a "crystal tower with light showers".

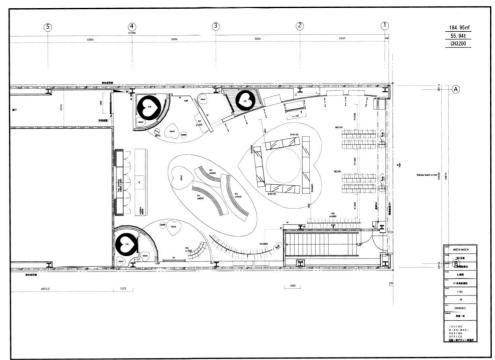

Floor Plan

MISCH MASCH (Tamaya co. ltd.) is a popular fashion brand targeting young women. The store we designed is a flagship store facing Shinsai-bashi shopping street, which is one of the most popular spots among the younger generation in Osaka. MISCH MASCH has already established a strong brand image with its 30 stores in shopping malls and department stores.

The store design concept is "magnificence" and "functionality". The Shinsai-bashi store is divided into two sections: front and rear; a large heart-shaped chandelier is set in the centre. "Heart" is the MISCH MASCH brand motif, so the chandelier represents the symbol of the store. It consists of limestones and Swarovski crystals and has CDM light source inside. With the illuminating CDM, the chandelier looks like a "crystal tower with light showers".

A wide counter is employed to enable sales people to assist multiple customers at the same time. At the side of the counter, there are large fitting rooms, in front of which, heart-shaped, original stools are arranged. It makes customers feel like being in a princess's room. Movable furniture is arranged under the chandelier provoking different atmospheres to the sales area. The store reinforces its own image and enhances the sales promotion.

Large fitting rooms with heart-shaped stools outside give customers the feeling of being in a princess's room.

Client
Tamaya Co. Ltd.

Design Team
Ichiro Nishiwaki, Takafumi Furuya, Makoto Yokochi

Main Contractor
Space

Lighting Consultant
Ushiospax

Lighting Fixtures & Fittings
Ushiospax, Crystal Fringe (heart chandelier) by East Village Gallery

Furniture
Stool from Adal Co.

Wall Covering
Di-noc film by Sumitomo 3M

Flooring
Advan Co.

Upholstery
Shaggy carpet by Poodle

Curtains/Blinds
Fringe by Simon Japan

Photography
Nacasa & Partners Inc.

Open, Hong Kong
Joey Ho Design

■ Hong Kong, China
■ 200 sq.m.

The designer plays upon the concept of spatial distortion manifested in the shop window and extends all the way into the shop interior.

© Mr. Graham Uden

© Mr. Graham Uden

The interior of this sports apparel shop aims at conveying a brand image that is both vibrant and stylish. The designer plays upon the concept of spatial distortion manifested in the shop window that extends all the way into the shop interior. In the shop window, mannequins are arranged on two planes, both horizontally and vertically. Lines and graphics radiate from the back of the shop window and further highlight the distorted dimension that customers are about to experience.

Inside, the distortion of space goes just about everywhere. Mannequins are turned upside down, angular benches and showcases unfold in all directions with metal sheets twist and turn to form functional display surfaces for running shoes. The use of black versus white adds to this illusory visual drama. There is a continuing displacement of surfaces, and a shift of planes which create a distorted impression as customers are led into different display zones. Rather than being static, the space evolves constantly, reinventing itself to illustrate and elaborate the dynamic image of the brand.

OPEN is a state of our mind... a wardrobe of style that is never closed.

The use of black versus white adds to the illusionary visual drama.

There is a continuing displacement of surfaces, and a shift of planes which create a distorted impression as customers are led into different display zones.

Client
Left & Right Limited

Design Team
Mr. Joey Ho

Main Contractor
GDA Design

Photography
Mr. Ray Lau, unless otherwise specified

PUMA Antwerp, Antwerp
Kanner Architects

■ **Antwerp, Germany**
■ **510 sq.m.**

A frameless glass and steel façade opens the
store's interior and merchandise to foot traffic
on the street.

Glass allows in natural light and minimizes the building's impact on the streetscape, which it was designed to complement.

An infill project in the historic Downtown area, PUMA Antwerp presented a number of design challenges that started with restoring the façade of a building that had been altered from its original character to another retail use. Responding to new historic preservation guidelines, Kanner Architects restored the façades of two storefronts that had been combined as a clothing store.

Because the restoration included the elimination of a canopy and the return of windows on the building's second level, Kanner Architects re-interpreted the canopy inside the store, with PUMA-red overhangs visible through the glass façade. These internal canopies serve as a visual cue of the street. They also serve as ceiling shells, marking the division of floors in a double-height space. Wrapping from the vertical walls into a lower ceiling, they also incorporate lighting and HVAC systems.

The frameless glass and steel façade opens the store's interior and merchandise to foot traffic on the street. The glass allows in natural light and minimizes the building's impact on the streetscape, which it was designed to complement. Per PUMA specs, the door is placed at the right end of the façade, welcoming visitors and directing them in the intended circulation pattern, through a series of merchandising zones that feature product in glass vitrines, and racks and shelves of metal and painted wood.

Once inside the store the PUMA brand principles emerge. The minimalist interior design is anchored by a red wall at the rear that creates a compelling focal point and draws consumers through the sales floor. The articulated walls and ceiling panels fold and flow over and around one another as well as existing structural columns. The

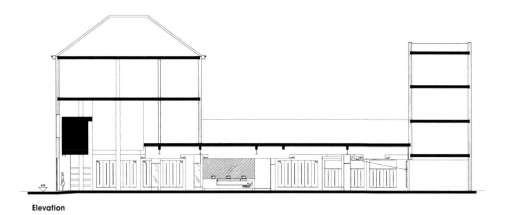

Elevation

Floor Plan

2 STORY HIGH SALES AREA

LANGE KLARENSTRAAT

SALES AREA

STOCK AREA

TYPICAL CEILING SHELL
ABOVE

180° DYLAN PROJECTION
IN RED WORLD SHOE AREA

effect is to create a concrete-floored archway that ties the building's original architecture into a contemporary design. The L-shaped forms and implied motion also represent the leaping cat of PUMA's logo. Bright red and white colours and clean lines finish the aesthetic.

Another of PUMA's Red World Elements is the fitting room, which is wallpapered to create unexpected scenarios - an elevator, the woods, a pantry - and feature a red curtain and a wall completely covered by a mirror.

A special feature in the Antwerp store is a projection system that shows PUMA mascot Dylan pouncing from wall to wall along a ledge above the merchandise.

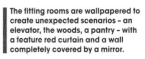

The fitting rooms are wallpapered to create unexpected scenarios – an elevator, the woods, a pantry – with a feature red curtain and a wall completely covered by a mirror.

Client
PUMA International

Design Team
Stephen H. Kanner (FAIA, Design Principal),
Nathan Colkitt, Claudia Wiehen,
Anna Yang

Photography
Jason Gray

Chinese Arts & Crafts Re-branding, Hong Kong
Panorama International Ltd.

- Hong Kong, China
- 275 sq.m.

The metaphor of interpreting the shopping space as a "Chinese Gift Box" was applied to promote different types of novelty gifts inside.

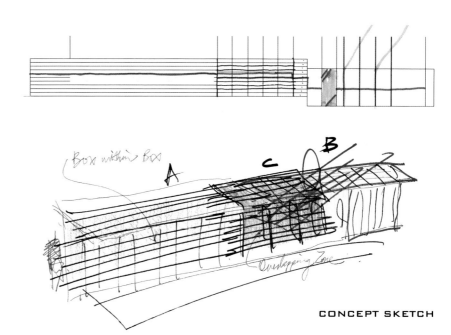

CONCEPT SKETCH

Chinese Arts & Crafts in JD Mall is the newest store recently launched by China Resources Retail (Group) Co., Ltd. in Hong Kong. It is a re-branding exercise to offer a diversified range of men's & ladies' apparels, antiques and a collection of novelty jewelleries - all of which would enhance the revitalization of Chinese arts.

The adopted interior design strategy was to re-interpret the brand identity by re-visiting the potential Chinese aesthetic elements in a contemporary way. To achieve this, the metaphor of interpreting the shopping space as a "Chinese Gift Box" was applied to promote different types of novelty gifts inside.

A dark spatial envelope made up of charcoal grey carpeting and exposed ceiling were firstly set up to provide an understated backdrop to the space. This was followed by a rectilinear composition of grids in both 2D and 3D provocations.

To echo the narrow and long spatial characteristics of the site, rectilinear display arrangements in the 3 key zones' and light systems were adopted. The prevailing "Chinese" personalities of the retail space were capitalized in both aesthetic and functional layers.

At the 1st compartment - the Jewellery zone, a feature wall-cum-ceiling made of golden, marble-patterned plastic fins created the texture of the "1st compartment" within the big gift box. Rows of golden yellow concealed light troughs reinforced the horizontality of this zone and subtly linked up the 1st & 2nd compartments.

Adjustable down spot lights brought focal attention to the fine jewellery (diamond & jade) items in the dimmed environment. Floating window display showcases with moving red LED lighting gave a glamorous/chic touch which symbolized an inter-weaving "red ribbon" on top of a gift box.

Grid displayed language in the Antique zone of the 2nd compartment was the result of the overlap between the horizontality and verticality of the 1st & 3rd compartments. They became horizontal glazed shelves and glowing vertical dividers of the wall units. Central full height glazed "pavilion" display showcases became the focus of the zone and provided opportunities for customers to look at the antiques in a 3-dimensional way.

The interplay of grid elements was finally completed with the glowing "wrapping paper" walls and ceiling in the 3rd compartment of the Apparel zone. Custom-made translucent monogram patterned glass was diffused by golden ambient light to reinforce a nostalgic mood. The system of free-standing/ceiling-suspended stainless steel hanger frameworks expressed the verticality and played the role of spatial dividers which penetrated into the apparel zone and floated the merchandise to the eyes of customers.

Rows of golden yellow concealed light troughs reinforce the horizontality of this zone and subtly link up the 1st & 2nd compartments.

Rows of golden yellow concealed light troughs reinforce the horizontality of this zone and subtly link up the 1st & 2nd compartments.

Central full height glazed "pavilion" display showcases became the focus of the zone and provided opportunities for customers to look at the antiques in a 3-dimensional way.

The interplay of grid elements was finally completed with the glowing "wrapping paper" walls and ceiling in the 3rd compartment of the Apparel zone.

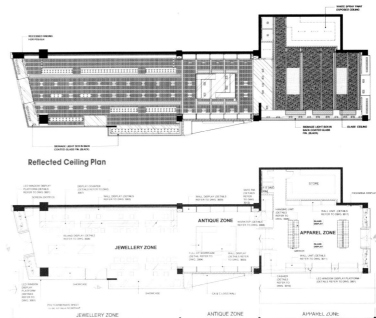

Reflected Ceiling Plan

Furniture Layout Plan

JEWELLERY ZONE | ANTIQUE ZONE | APPAREL ZONE

Client
Chinese Arts & Crafts (HK) Ltd.

Design Team
Horace Pan, Alan Tse, Vivian Chan

Main Contractor
Sentech Design & Construction Co., Ltd.

Photography
Ng Siu Fung

Voyage, London
Blacksheep

■ London, U. K.
■ 205 sq.m.

To create a 'distressed' look on the walls, three different types of paint were used. In a 'trial and test' scenario, the paints were treated with a belt sander until they created a 'reveal' effect.

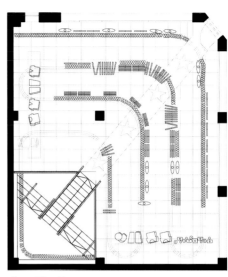

Ground Floor Plan

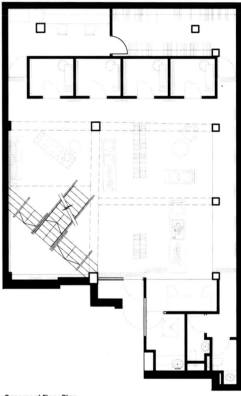

Basement Floor Plan

Blacksheep created a two-level London flagship store for cult Italian fashion label Voyage on London's newly-burgeoning Conduit Street, where Vivienne Westwood, Moschino and the hugely-influential bar/ restaurant/ nightclub Sketch have all found a home in recent times.

Owners Tatum and Rocky Mazzilli, daughter and son of the original founders of the Voyage label (Tiziano and Louise Mazzilli), had leased a premium site on the corner of Conduit Street and Savile Row, but didn't have much time to implement a new design concept – or a huge budget to achieve it. Looking for highly creative, ingenious but cost-effective ideas, Tatum and Rocky had already seen a number of design groups before being introduced to Blacksheep, whose loose and theatrical concepts, enthusiasm and willingness to be inventive with the budget went down a storm.

The overall theme of the new store was a highly theatrical and eclectic presentation space, where, like an art gallery, themed installations could transform the space at regular – or irregular – intervals.

Two huge glass windows allow passers-by great views into the interior. Central to the interior concept was the use, throughout the ground floor, of a standard and low-cost theatrical ceiling rail, usually used as heavy-duty rigging for stage curtains, which allowed clothes to be hung, moved and changed on a whim and allowed for great flexibility of presentation. Merchandise hangs off the rail in a variety of ways, including clothing hung against orange and sheer backdrops and on suspended rails with specially made hangers in red flocked material. The effect is dramatic, but approachable, removing the inaccessibility of much couture clothing presentation techniques.

The 'industrial' feel of the rails is complemented by spot-lighting on a ceiling track grid, set against a midnight-blue ceiling, like a starscape – inspired by a Jimi Hendrix album cover! The ground-floor flooring is limestone, inset with a spectacular red Sicilian marble 'runway' and featuring four large cream marble stars, echoing the celebrity inset stars of LA's Sunset Boulevard. To the rear of the 'runway' and in the far corner of the store, a large dark red velvet backdrop curtain draws customers' attention to the stair leading down to the lower-ground floor.

To create a 'distressed' look on the walls, three different types of paint were used. In a 'trial and test' scenario, the paints were treated with a belt sander until they created a great 'reveal' effect. This raw feel is offset by the treatment of the support columns, where vintage wallpapers were overlaid one onto another and then torn back to achieve a parallel 'revealed' look.

Freestanding furniture on the ground floor area includes one-off 20th century design classic chairs (such as Eero Aarnio's 1968 hanging 'Bubble' chair), from the Mazzillis' private collection, and generous-scale freestanding mirrors, to encourage people to see how they look – and to feel free to pose! - in Voyage's clothes.

The ground floor's stunning red-lit cashdesk (with lights left on at night to attract attention from passing club- and bar-goers), was the result of a spontaneous on-site idea. Some light trays were accidentally left behind on site by the previous tenenat. Blacksheep took these, gelled them red and used them as the frontispiece of the new 'hotspot' cashdesk.

For the lower-ground floor, a parallel but different theme was created. Customers are led down a stair covered in stencilled slogans such as tongue-in-cheek 'say yes to botox' and the self-ironic 'say no to membership'. Here,

the space is darker, along the lines of a star's boudoir, creating a more intimate and luxurious feel, with darker flooring in chocolate limestone setting the tone. This space was also designed for the Mazzillis to host parties, and includes decent male and female toilets and a 'gentleman's bar' area. The floor, which also includes concealed stock room and small office space, is the same footprint as the ground floor above.

Dominating one entire wall are four generously-proportioned changing rooms, based on the idea of on-set movie star Winnebagos. Each 'wannabe Winnebago' changing room has a silver-grey metallic exterior and a door with a 'star' graphic on an opaque glass inset. For the interior of each changing room, the Mazzillis wanted to use vintage wallpaper. After a long search, Blacksheep tracked down an east London builder's merchant with a small range of left-over wallpapers from the last 40 years. The final choices were papers from children's films – one for each changing room, including

Snow White, 101 Dalmations, Ninja Turtles and Super Mario. Further vintage papers were used to clad the support columns, which, echoing the ground floor columns, were layered with different papers and then 'distressed'.

Individual items of furniture on this floor include a leather chair, which had been worn to reveal the stuffing (Blacksheep then covered the overflowing stuffing with silk to make it look as though it was silk overflowing) and a standard lamp, customised with antique chandelier lighting. Art pieces, such as a giant-sized basket of eggs, serve as eye-catching installations and are also for sale.

Merchandising on the lower ground floor is more spare, contrasting with the ground floor, with individual items displayed on hooks set into the walls of the changing room.

A low-cost theatrical ceiling
rail allows cltohes to be hung,
moved and changed on a whim
and allows for great flexibilitiy of
presentation.

Client
Tatum and Rocky Mazzilli

Main Contractor
Talina

Lighting Consultant
Kate Wilkins

Consultant
Ian Thomson MRICS

Structural Consultant
Fluid Structures: David Crooks

AV Consultant
Orbital Sounds Limited

Steel Work
M & G Steel Fabrications

Theater Track
Harkness Hall Ltd.

Artwork
Signage by Blaze Neon Limited

Photography
Edmund Sumner

Virgin Megastore, Manchester
Checkland Kindleysides

- Manchester, U.K.
- 1,635 sq.m.

'Gig' style flight cases on wheels are a key merchandising feature; reminiscent of the band on tour, they give the impression of a store that is constantly changing and on the move.

The brief was to design a new concept for Virgin Megastores; creating a destination store that would bring entertainment to the fore.

Capturing the unique energy and pioneering spirit of both Sir Richard Branson and the Virgin brand, we created a new store concept for Virgin Megastore which engages and inspires the consumer and brings interactive entertainment to life.

Immersive interactive 'Hubs' allow consumers to truly experience Virgin's music, DVD and gaming offer (one 'hub' for each). Each has its own distinct colour taken from the Virgin palette, red for Digital (music), theatrical black for DVD and an energetic vibrant yellow for the Games hub. Acting as beacons across the store, they form destination points where consumers can meet, relax and sample the latest releases.

Graphics infuse the personality and warmth of the Virgin brand, from gritty black and white imagery of iconic Mancunian heroes, which connect the store to its Manchester location and give it an independent feel, to the 'Virgin Voice' graphic language which uses 'speech bubbles' to enable consumers to navigate the store with ease.

'Gig' style flight cases on wheels are a key merchandising feature; reminiscent of the band on tour, they give the impression of a store that is constantly changing and on the move. These are used throughout the store to highlight everything from the coolest 12" vinyl to the freshest new releases.

Further blurring the line between retail and entertainment, the 230 sq. m. basement, with its 'indie club' feel (which has been likened to the legendary

'100 Club'), hosts gigs from major artists to unsigned hopefuls. Here, 'gig ticket' covered walls enhance the club feel. Even in the toilets, speech bubbles with iconic Manc's lyrics playfully continue the theme.

We sculpted the store with sound and light. Using a zone system to create walls of sound, changing from inside to outside the 'hubs'. Lighting was also used to create a different atmosphere in each 'hub' and add a contemporary softness across the store, whilst highlighting key promotions and graphics.

The store is achieving its objective of moving the brand back to the core Virgin heritage, 'Virgin-ness' has been injected back into the Megastore.

Immersive interactive 'Hubs' allow
consumers to truly experience
Virgin's music, DVD and gaming
offer, each with its own distinct
colour taken from the Virgin
palette.

Client
Virgin Retail Ltd.

Main Contractor
CG Interiors

Lighting Consultant
Prolight

Art Consultant
Checkland Kindleysides

Lighting Fixtures & Fittings
Prolight

Furniture
Bespoke Merchandising by Checkland
Kindleysides
Standard Furniture by Resolution Interiors

AV System
Impact Marcom
Listening Posts by Hobert Computing
GmbH

Photography
Keith Parry

Boboo, Xi'an
JBM Design

■ **Xi'an, China**
■ **600 sq.m.**

A large window display allows for flexibility in changing the display paterns for all seasonal and festive events.

The mission statement of Boboo is: Strategy, Management, Image, Service, Pricing, and Marketing. Their goal is to deliver the complexity of management with a universal corporate and visual identity. This enables Boboo to be ranked the number one casual wear in Mainland China.

Boboo first approached the designer to revamp their existing localized image and turn it into a stylish and trendy upbeat image. Their target group is the well-educated young generation who possesses a strong sense of personal style and identity.

At the shop front, the designer combined LED screens with lighting effects to strengthen the brand image and provoke a prevailing sensation of mystery. A large window display is installed to replace the typical narrow shop front design. The intention is to allow flexibility in changing the display patterns for all seasonal and festive events.

The interior space provides multiple visual and tactile levels. By utilizing the elevated ceiling, the designer creates a focal point of a curved, wooden ceiling that contrasts with the wooden hollow screens. Contemporary design elements are added throughout the revamp project.

By utilizing the elevated ceiling, the designer creates a focal point of a curved, wooden ceiling that contrasts with wooden hollow screens.

Client
Boboo

Design Team
Michael Chan

Photography
JBM Design

Style Hong Kong, Chengdu
Joseph Sy & Associates

- Chengdu, China
- 300 sq.m.

Dominated by theatrical lights with bold colours and a curved geometry, the layout brings out a young and spirited vitality to the area.

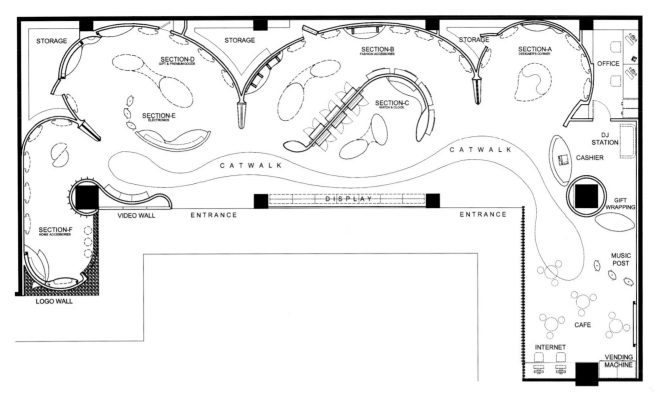

Floor Plan

Style Hong Kong Shop is a promotional platform for the Hong Kong Trade and Development Council to nourish the Chinese market on state-of-the art designer items created in Hong Kong. Its design has created a fun, free flowing, organic and casual ambiance for the display items throughout the store.

Because of the diversity of products it sells, flexibility is the key element in the shop making it akin to a small department store. In line with this consideration, the whole display combination can be reorganized, depending on the needs or themes at different times.

Shelf arrangements are strategic, wherein the shelves at the central aisle are set at mid height and the wall shelving at full height so that the supervisory staff can have an overview of the whole shop at a glance and monitor the areas easily.

Dominated by theatrical lights with bold colours and curved geometry, the layout brings out a young and spirited vitality to the area, and at the same time, manages to highlight the distinctive personalities of each of the collection produced by its designer.

Other features include a video wall with a continuous stream of informational updates on designers, their products and upcoming HKTDC events; there is also a café/lounge area where one can enjoy a brief break during shopping spree.

All the design elements and considerations mentioned above are brought about by basic materials which reveal the fact that an innovative shop design to showcase true creativity and usefulness does not necessarily be expensive.

Ever since the opening of Mainland markets for free enterprise and the growth in consumption power, there has been a great demand for designer products made in Hong Kong. Mainland consumers consider Hong Kong products as the template for quality and class. The Style Hong Kong Shop captures this demand; and at the same time promotes a kind of upwardly mobile and free lifestyle which effectively influences the priorities and perceptions of its target market and helps in elevating the cultural adaptation to a modern, cosmopolitan movement at par with Hong Kong and other major cities of the world.

Centre aisle shelves are set
at mid height and the wall
shelving at full height so that
supervisorial staff can view the
whole shop at a glance.

Main Contractor
Seaview Contracting Ltd.

Lighting Consultant
Joseph Sy & Associates

Photography
Joseph Sy

Paradies Shops at the Georgia Aquarium, Georgia
TVS Interiors

Georgia, U.S.A.
610 sq.m.

Internally illuminated fabric forms weave rhythmically through the space while obscuring the irregular column placement.

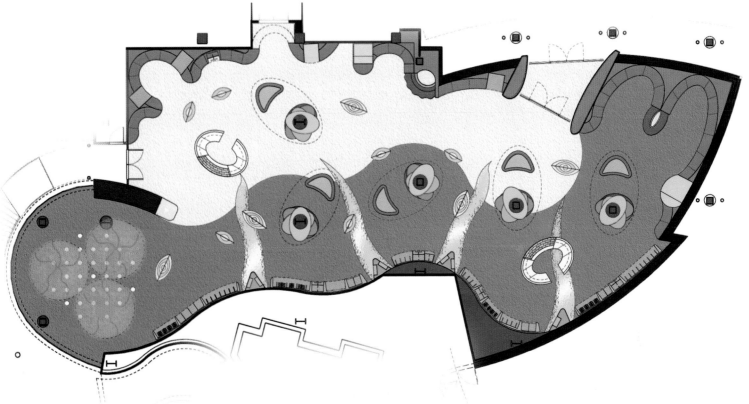

Floor Plan

Located in Atlanta, Georgia, the Paradies Shops at the Georgia Aquarium are an aquatic extension of the five galleries featured throughout the attraction. To create an innovative shopping environment, the Aquarium's largest gift shop was designed to produce an immersive experience of an underwater swim in an ocean of sea creatures, souvenirs and memorabilia from the Aquarium's attractions.

Located at the end of the fifth gallery, the first and largest shop, the 6,000 sq. ft. "Beyond the Reef" welcomes visitors to a darkened deep-sea environment complete with glimmering jellies and large tendrils of green kelp, which climb and twist to form passageways. Internally illuminated fabric forms weave rhythmically through the space while obscuring the irregular column placement. The sparkling terrazzo

floor replicates the ambience of a Technicolor ocean floor glittering with shells and rock fragments. At the point of sale, a stylized coral wall creates the illusion of an underwater reef, complete with cracks and crevices – an illusion heightened through the imaginative use of theatrical lighting and plasma screens featuring oceanographic video. The fixtures on which merchandise is displayed are freestanding sculptures of marine life.

The second store, Sandollar, is a 600 sq. ft. children's nook where tension-hung shelving displays merchandise in such a way that it appears to be suspended in water. Pale blue and yellow terrazzo flooring and a lime-green ceiling glowing with jellyfish-like lights create a cheerful space in which children can interact with "sea creatures".

Overall these spaces are mysterious and intriguing, which invite visitors in and encourage them to discover even more about the world's ocean creatures. Colourful and playful, the Paradies Shops at the Georgia Aquarium are both unique in design and successful in their purpose to encourage the sale of merchandise.

Glimmering jellies and large
tendrils of green kelp, which climb
and twist to form passageways.

Client
Paradies Shops

Design Team
Steve Clem, Paula Carr, Dana Carter

Main Contractor
Brasfield & Gorrie

Architect
TVS

Lighting Consultant
Bliss Fasman

Lighting Fixtures & Fittings
Juno Lighting

Wall Covering
Venetian plaster by Goodman

Flooring
Solid Surfacing by Avonite,
Terrazzo by US Mosaic

Millwork/Cabinetry
Raydeo Enterprises

Fixtures
ALU

Exhibit Fixtures
Raydeo Enterprises

Photography
Brian Gassel

STEPHANE DOUCHANGLEEYUGIN

Stephane Dou Changlee Yugin Tiger City, Taichung

CJ Studio

■ Taichung, Taiwan
■ 130 sq.m.

This showroom for the Taiwan fashion designers is a re-interpretation of the relationship between fashion and architecture.

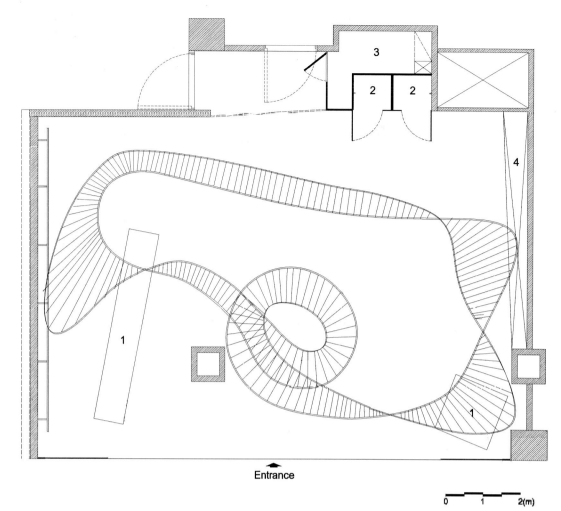

Floor Plan:- 1 Showcase; 2 Dress; 3 Storage; 4 Counter

Entrance

0 1 2(m)

This showroom for Taiwan fashion designer Stephane Dou and Changlee Yugin is a re-interpretation of the relationship between fashion and architecture. It is an installation which represents the function and spatial experience simultaneously. This installation consists of two interwoven lines made by polished stainless steel. The surface between the two lines is fixed and stretched by threads. Therefore, the installation becomes a field of display and provides a dynamic system. In order to reflect the client's view of fashion, the wall and the floor are made of alumni panels, which express a cold but resplendent feeling. The installation can accommodate the great demand in clothes hanging. At the same time, customers can enjoy shopping and view this installation as if they were walking into a museum. It is time for celebrating the shopping fun.

STEPHANE DOU CHANG LEE YUGIN

Client
Stephane Dou & Changlee Yugin

Design Team
Shichieh Lu

Photography
Kuomin Lee

Sirius Praha, Prague
Maurice Mentjens Design

- Prague, Czech Republic
- 78 sq.m.

Glass bell-jars on the wall around the doorway to
the larger room, store the "magic potions" sold
at Sirius, called the "smart products".

Sirius Praha is a "smart shop" and a record store housed in a typical 18th century building behind the National Theatre of Prague. The rooms are characterised by the barrel vaulting so typical of many buildings in the Czech Republic dated from that era.

In 1995, my first shop interior for Sirius in Maastricht was designed as an alchemistic laboratory. The interiors for the Sirius stores in Roermond and Eindhoven (both at 1996) were based on alchemistic themes. I took the same theme as the basis for the design in Prague.

The laboratory in Maastricht represents the scientific aspect of alchemy while the spiritual aspect is portrayed in Roermond. Then comes Eindhoven, representing the alchemistic process or the Opus

Magnum, and finally the preparation of the Philosopher's Stone or gold (or spiritual gold). I wanted to bring the last phase of this process to a kind of completion in Prague.

In the middle of the space in the shop in Eindhoven stands a black stone surrounded by the full spectrum of the rainbow. In Prague, this stone colour changes to gold. The interior in Prague is completely white, with a counter that is literally both black and gold. As you enter through the front door, the counter is black, but as you walk towards the next room, it turns into gold. This effect has been created by using a special varnish, known as flip-flop lacquer. Depending on the viewer's location, the counter is either gold or black. Here, too, the completely white space can take on thousands of colours, albeit as a uniform-coloured glow of light.

Here, the completely white space can take on thousands of colours, albeit as a uniform-coloured glow of light.

In this space, we also see glass bell-jars on the wall around the doorway to the larger room, under which are stored the "magic potions" sold at Sirius, called the "smart products".

The square niches behind the counter are used for the storage of records and as a display wall for new releases. In the room next door are three large record racks, arranged in parallel to each other. By laying a sheet of glass on top of one of these racks, it can be turned into a display case for DJ requisites.

The back wall is covered with mirrors, making the room look much larger. On this wall is a long DJ table, with five turntables and spaces for the records to be listened to. Above the DJ table, a large circle hovers like an aureole with a dot in the middle symbolizing eternity, which in combination with the dot represents the unity of

a macro and micro cosmos. A large ring shape has been sanded away in the mirror behind which are fluorescent tube light fittings to produce the lighting effect.

Both rooms are illuminated by a large metal beam hanging from the middle of the ceiling. This beam continues right through the wall, and seems to form a construction that is supported by the metal frame around the doorway.

The beam contains three coloured fluorescent lamps (red, green and blue), with which thousands of colours can be created, but if all lights are switched on, it will produce white illumination.

I wanted to create a lattice of metal discs with a diameter of 25mm on the walls and on the vaulted ceiling. Magnets can be

Both rooms are illuminated by a large metal beam hanging from the middle of the ceiling. This beam continues right through the wall, and seems to form a construction that is supported by the metal frame around the doorway.

attached to these discs, so that records, CDs and T-shirts etc. can be displayed on the walls and ceiling.

For budgetary reasons, these metal discs will be added at a later stage. For the same reason, the counter is currently covered with golden laminate instead of spray-painted with flip-flop lacquer. This will also be brought into line with the design at a later stage.

Above the DJ table, a large circle hovers like an aureole with a dot in the middle symbolizing eternity.

Client
Sirius Smart Sounds

Main Contractor
Robert Bellada Nabytek

Electric Installation
Jiří Lonský, Elektro – Servis

Counter Finish
HPL Golden laminate

AV System
Amps by Douwe Medema

Photography
Veva van Sloun

Kitson Men, California
Space International Inc.

■ California, U.S.A.
■ 232 sq.m.

The storefront addresses the captured image through a variety of "framing devices", and attempts to blur the line between private and public territories.

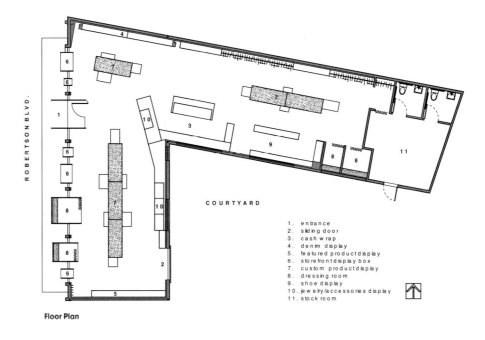

Floor Plan

1 . entrance
2 . sliding door
3 . cash wrap
4 . denim display
5 . featured product display
6 . storefront display box
7 . custom product display
8 . dressing room
9 . shoe display
10 . jewelry/accessories display
11 . stock room

Self described as the favourite shop for the "who's who" in Hollywood, and often acting as a media spot for paparazzi and celebrity encounters, this high profile boutique maintains a unique relationship with celebrities. The design for the men's store is focused on "articulating" the sometimes conspicuously consuming habit associated with window shopping, star tracking and voyeurism in today's community. The storefront addresses the captured image through a variety of "framing devices", and attempts to blur the line between private and public territories by allowing these envelopes to subtly transgress conventional boundaries.

Here, the products and patrons are put on display as captured moments through undulating steel volumes which serve as billboards and blinders simultaneously. Programmed for the entrance, display, and dressing rooms, all elements which represent public and private are diffused into forms of exhibition.

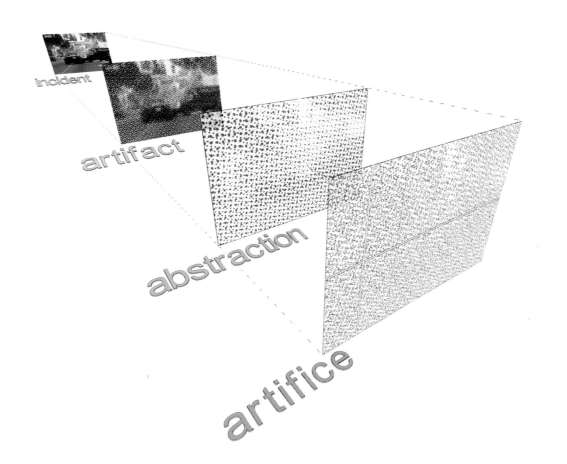

incident

artifact

abstraction

artifice

View through dressing room.

Client
Kitson

Main Contractor
Bonura Builders

Lighting Consultant
Space International Inc.

Lighting Fixtures & Fittings
DaSal Industries, Delray Lighting, W.A.C.
Lighting, Artemide Inc.

Furniture
Space International Inc.

Wall Covering
A.R.G. Acrylics

Photography
Joshua White

Kiki 2, Maastricht
Maurice Mentjens Design

■ **Maastricht, The Netherlands**
■ **34 sq.m.**

The shop is designed as a warehouse with walls and ceilings covered with racks and cabinets in grey oak wood, giving it an old and dusty appeal.

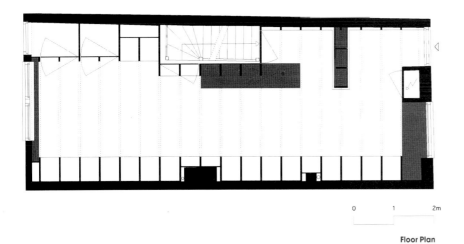

0   1   2m

Floor Plan

Kiki 2 is the outlet shop of Kiki Niesten located in a 16th century building at the heart of Maastricht. Kiki wanted a functional yet subtly chic, luxurious, and witty shop, something that embraces jokes. They also required a lot of storage space in the fairly small shop with its high ceiling.

The shop is designed as a warehouse with walls and ceilings covered with racks and cabinets in grey oak wood, which gives it an old and dusty appeal.

The floor is covered with white clothes scattered across the floor and cast in completely transparent epoxy resin. It looks as if a client, in a state of 'shopping delirium', pulled everything out of the cabinets.

Light is emitted through a box pending over the counter, which conceals the staircase leading to the first floor. The door to this staircase is hidden behind a secret door to the left of the counter, concealed behind the cabinets with mirrors at the back.

A large glass walled cabinet next to the counter acts as a barrier to the back of the counter and blocks the direct draft when the front door is open. At the rear of the shop, two dressing rooms are fitted in to the cabinet walls on the same side as the counter. It is possible to hang clothing from three separate levels, and shelves can also be placed in all cabinets.

Finally, two ladders with the same wood finish as the cabinets are made to reach the higher shelves.

The floor is covered with white clothes scattered across the floor and cast in completely transparent epoxy resin.

Client
Kiki Niesten Maastricht

Main Contractor
Interieurbouw Hees, Echt

Floor Conultant
Paul ten Hoeve, Etienne Reijnders

Lighting Fixtures & Fittings
Halogen Spotlights and Lamps

Furniture
Oakwood Veneer

Ceiling
Oakwood Veneer

Flooring
Epoxy resin and white clothes

Photography
Arjen Schmitz

Epic, Nevada
AkarStudios

■ Nevada, U.S.A.
■ 60 sq.m.

The store's minimal interior has the feel of a gallery,

exhibiting the latest in urban footwear.

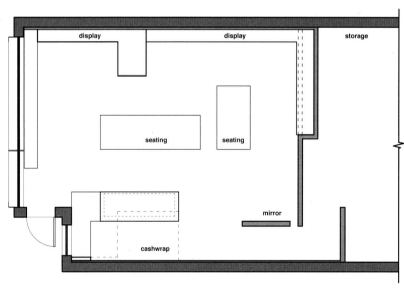

Floor Plan

Located on Main Street in the up-and-coming Arts District of Downtown Las Vegas, which has been forging a new social culture with venues for the fashion conscious elite, tourists and urbanites, the designers transformed this rundown storefront space into a sleek, contemporary, urban boutique, giving this fast developing area one of its first true retail destinations. The client's brief was quite simple, geared around the practical requirements of the space and creating a sensory experience, similar to that of an art gallery, for the display of casual sneakers on the walls.

From the street, the exterior appears as a minimal intervention into the existing commercial fabric. The façade has been given a simple contemporary facelift, with new storefront glazing and a new paint job. At night, the retail space glows like a beacon of urban sophistication, drawing curious shoppers in from the street. Of the 2,300 sq. ft. lease space, the showroom display space occupies an area of approximately 700 sq. ft. The balance of the space has been left for storage and future expansion.

The store's minimal interior has the feel of a gallery, exhibiting the latest in urban footwear with a sculptural display element of dark walnut wood that wraps continuously through the space. A low, oversized bench divides the store, providing a vantage point from which one can view the entire collection displayed on the walls. The retail space is visually separated from the rear storage area by a large, floor-to-ceiling photographic mural that is visible from the sidewalk. Recessed within the plane of this graphic wall is a backlit niche highlighting the shop's latest offerings.

Completing the store's identity as an oasis of urban cool in the Vegas desert, the cash-wrap counter houses a glass-door refrigerator, stocked with mineral water and Gatorade bottles for customers taking a break from the heat in the crisp, refreshing atmosphere of this retail destination.

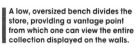

A low, oversized bench divides the store, providing a vantage point from which one can view the entire collection displayed on the walls.

Client
Todd Burden

Design Team
Sat Garg (Principal),
Matt Lutz (Project Designer)

Lighting Consultant
AkarStudios

Lighting Fixtures & Fittings
Liton, Los Angeles, CA

Furniture
LA Construction

Artwork
AkarStudios

Photography
Derek Rath

Nuance Duty Free, Ontario
Mackay|Wong Strategic Design

- Ontario, Canada
- 1,020 sq.m.

High impact colours, materials, feature lighting and strategically planned shopping districts form a retail environment that is fresh, modern and highly successful.

Serving in excess of 30,000 passengers per day, Toronto's highly acclaimed new airport terminal has set very high standards of design. The airport's architectural character projects a sophisticated international style that avoids regional clichés. Bright and modern, the terminal makes an excellent backdrop for creative retail and restaurant facilities offered throughout.

In collaboration with Airport Design Group, Mackay|Wong developed a new interiors prototype concept for the client's Duty Free business. Gone are the typical stale aisles of over-merchandised display units and poorly lit surfaces. Together, high impact colours, materials, feature lighting and strategically planned shopping districts with organized brand placement form a retail environment that is fresh, modern and highly successful.

This 11,000 sq. ft. location is our client's premium location with sales volumes which are 25% higher than their best performing stores throughout North America.

Handbag display

Makeup display

Client
Pearson International Airport

Consultant
Airport Design Group

Photography
David Whittaker

Sony Ericsson Flagship Store, London
Checkland Kindleysides

- London, U.K.
- 360 sq.m.

The concept uses architecturally simple and beautiful ergonomic forms to create a cool and contemporary retail environment.

The brief was to design Sony Ericsson's first ever store, reflecting the new direction of the brand as it enters a phase of aggressive growth. This new direction is about creating an engaging environment that will encourage a broader range of consumers to interact with the Sony Ericsson brand.

Our concept uses architecturally simple and beautiful ergonomic forms to create a cool and contemporary retail environment, reflective of the design philosophy of this Japanese / Swedish brand. Drawing on the corporate branding and accessible non-technical language, the product is conveyed with clarity to the consumer and celebrates the product as a 'hero'.

Providing movement and impact on the high street, the colour changing fascia echoes the Sony Ericsson's brand palette and

changes in sequence with the lighting used in store on both the central handset display and perimeter merchandising.

Forming the focal point and central architectural reference to the store, is the 'infinity' bar, a sculpted demonstration and service bar which runs the length of the store.

Divided into three sections, the bar presents Sony Ericsson's full range of handsets. The first section of the bar celebrates the future and showcases the latest models. All phones on display are live and connected, with touch screen plasmas recessed into the bar offering additional product information, and providing consumers with a truly interactive and engaging experience. Electrically alarmed recoilers provide power and security to the handsets effectively and discreetly. The central section includes online

more music

it!

more power

access, encouraging the consumer to spend time with the products and learn about their functionality. The final section is a serviced area showcasing products dedicated to the business user.

The perimeter merchandising is angled, generating customer flow through the store whilst highlighting accessories on sale. Around the store large colourful graphics show close ups of products set against a bold coloured background selected from the brand colour palette, alone with messages from the new brand language.

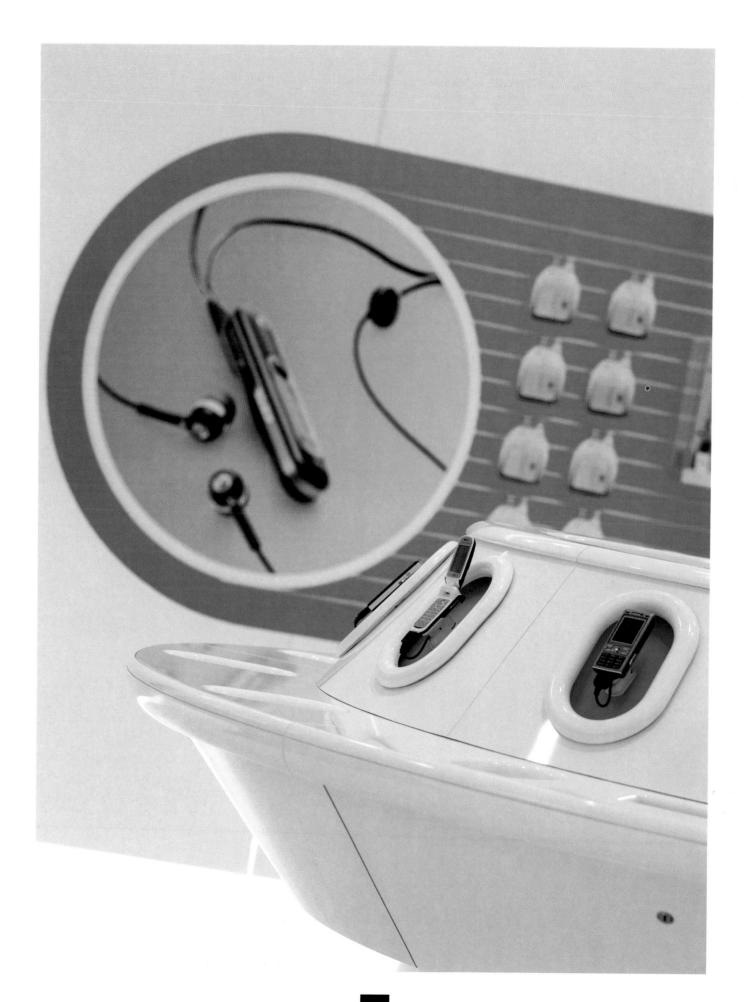

Client
Sony Ericsson

Main Contractor
Oakwood Shopfitting

Phone Security
Phone security recoilerys - Stacey Security

Photography
Keith Parry

POSH Showroom - Central, Hong Kong
POSH Marketing Team

- Hong Kong, China
- 280 sq.m.

POSH seeks to replace the cool, dull, commercial image of an office furniture store with an environmentally friendly, natural, and cosy design.

POSH is an environmentally conscious furniture store with 20% of their products being from overseas designers and the rest from their own R+D team in China. They wanted to replace the idea of a cool, dull, commercial image of an office furniture store with a more environmentally friendly, natural, fresh, and cosy design.

To reflect their consciousness and their motto of "Better design, better environment" their green company logo is translated into a faux grass high wall feature inside the store. This connection to nature is enhanced with a waterfall-like screen, made of white silk, at the front of the store and pebbles at the base of raised wooden levels at the display window.

As the main idea of a showroom is to display its products to its best advantage, the POSH showroom is set up in several arrangements to enhance its unity while the entrance is located at the right of the store to maximize the usable showroom space.

On the walls above each arrangement of office furniture is a large hanging backdrop depicting the look, feel, and possibilities of the furniture. LED frames that change colour give a more in depth, layered view, and at night, when the store is closed, act along with the lights at the store front to grab the attention of passers by.

Client
POSH Office Systems (HK) Ltd.

Design Team
POSH Marketing Team

Photography
Courtesy of POSH Office Systems

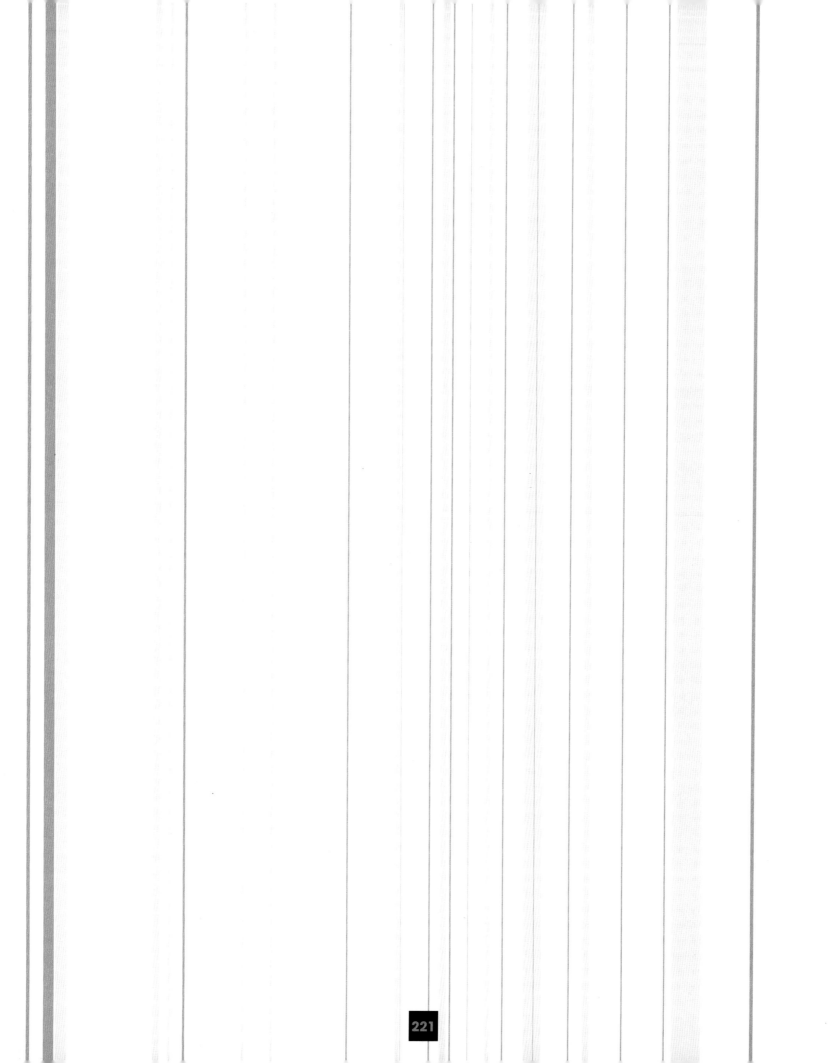

Acknowledgements

pace publishing limited wishes to acknowledge the support of the following individuals and their respective organizations in providing materials for this publication.

Andrea Wilson | II BY IV Design Associates Inc.
Pal Pang | Another
Mei Ling Moore | AkarStudios
Roslyn Campbell | Blacksheep
Michelle Auer | burdifilek
Abigail Lloyd-Jones | Checkland Kindleysides
Athena | CJ Studio
Sofie Ruytenberg | Concrete Architectural Associates
Akiyo Fujii | GLAMOROUS co., ltd.
Eri Takahashi | Ichiro Nishiwaki Design Office Inc.
Margaret Chan | JBM Design
Su Lau | Joey Ho Design
Yan Wong | Joseph Sy & Associates
Christopher Keough | Kanner Architects
Kathy Grant | Mackay|Wong Strategic Design
Yume Dannenburg | Maurice Mentjens Design
Horace Pan | Panorama International Ltd.
Lam Lam | POSH Mareting Team
John Hirsch | Space International Inc.
Jennie Coakley | TVS Interiors